# Summary and Analysis of "Talk Like TED: 9 Public-Speaking Secrets of the World's Top Minds" by Carmine Gallo

*Summary Station*

Copyright © 2014 by Summary Station

All rights reserved. This book or any portion thereof may not be reproduced or used in any manner whatsoever without the express written permission of the publisher except for the use of brief quotations in a book review.

Printed in the United States of America

First Printing, 2014

# Table of Contents

What is TED? ................................................................................4
Chapter 1- Unleash the Master Within ...............................................5
Chapter 2- Master the Art of Storytelling ...........................................9
Chapter 3: Have A Conversation ......................................................12
Chapter 4: Teach Me Something New ...............................................16
Chapter 5: Deliver Jay-Dropping Moments .......................................20
Chapter 7: Stick to the 18-Minute Rule ............................................29
Chapter 8: Paint a Mental Picture with Multisensory Experiences ..33
Chapter 9: Stay In Your Lane ..........................................................37
Thanks for Reading ........................................................................40
About Summary Station ..................................................................41
Preview of "Summary and Analysis of "The Slight Edge" by Jeff Olson"" ..........................................................................................43
Check Out More Books By Summary Station ...................................46

# What is TED?

TED – Technology, Education, Design – is an extensive compilation of presentations and interviews of TED's most prominent and innovative professionals. People of all backgrounds and careers have implemented the TED method in their respective markets. "Talk Like TED" takes you on a journey through each key concept necessary to reap the proven scientific benefits of the TED method. Broken into three parts, Carmine Gallo, uses examples from interactions with dozens of TED's finest presenters, taking you on a journey toward becoming an inspirational, life-changing, impacting, legendary speaker.

# Chapter 1- Unleash the Master Within

This chapter begins with an amazing story of how Aimee Mullins did more than overcome adversity, she triumphed everything society thought they "knew" about the limits posed on an amputee. Mullins did not have lower legs since she was an infant. While she was disabled physically, mentally she became stronger. She learned to tap into her internal superpowers and unleash a master greater than the world had ever seen. In The 1996 Paralympics, Mullins broke three world records in track and field. Running for Georgetown University in a NCAA Division One program, she gained the skills to turn heads and drop jaws with her triple record-smashing feat.

If that wasn't admirable enough, Mullins went on to become a fashion model, actress, and even found a place on People Magazine's "50 Most Beautiful People" list. That's unleashing a master like no other. Mullins saw no limits, she never viewed herself as disabled or incapable, which allowed her to do the "impossible".

Her story leads to *Secret #1* listed in "Talk Like TED", the chapter's namesake **"Unleash The Master Within"**. When selecting a presentation topic, it's imperative to choose something unique that you hold a meaningful connection to. Passion is, without a doubt, a necessary emotion that will guide you towards identifying that mastery.

Science supports this claim with concrete evidence. Passion is contagious. The only way to create an inspirational presentation is by being inspired yourself.

Carmine Gallo explains how he interviews executives who are looking to become better communicators. Originally, he would first ask, "What are you passionate about?" This question got a response but it wasn't nearly as exciting and thought provoking as the answers to his revised question, "What makes your heart sing?"

Executives would share tales of how "The American Dream" affected their transition from immigrants to multi-millionaires. You're encouraged to ask yourself the same question. Take a moment to think before delivering an honest answer. Don't include hobbies or passive interests; force yourself to acknowledge what's intensely necessary to your identity. Then you need to question how much this passion influences your daily life. Is it possible to incorporate this passion into your profession?

From a temporary retreat in 2004, Matthieu Ricard left the Shechen Monastery only to be labeled the happiest man in the world. His TED talk covered his thoughts on how happiness is a "deep sense of serenity and fulfillment." After volunteering for a study at the University of Wisconsin, Madison, Ricard's brain waves were measured as the "happiest" in history. He didn't care about the title; he wanted everyone in the world to know they could be just as happy.

If you're speaking on a topic that makes your heart sing, your natural passion will make you happy, reduce nervousness, and your joy will become infectious. Not to be confused with making a sale or gaining higher status, true passion and receptiveness comes from motives that are more altruistic. If you're out to inspire people, help them to improve their lives, and are working towards the greater good of all, you'll reach a much broader audience. Without this natural happiness, it's likely you won't feel satisfied in your career.

Steve Jobs is frequently referenced throughout "Talk Like TED" due to his overwhelming passion for the topic. Overall, happiness is a choice in every aspect of life. Even challenges can be viewed as opportunities. It's all a matter of perspective.

Passion and presentations go hand-in-hand if you want to make an impact. Numerous studies and examples of TED presentations are referenced to prove that fact. From working in areas like under-served urban environments, domestic violence, even neuropathy, when associated with first-hand experiences that fuel your passion, these commonly discussed topics will really stand out.

Your level of passion isn't limited to personal thoughts and feelings. It's very important to surround yourself with equally passionate people. Working alongside similarly inspired minds, anything is possible.

Don't let your drive outshine your purpose. Silence is a forgotten art form, especially when dealing with "experts" and professionals. The brain is always growing and your perspective is always expanding, the only way to be sure you're collecting and presenting accurate facts is by being willing to sit back and observe. Learn from your environment before jumping in and changing things, this way you'll be able to formulate the best way to approach your analysis.

# Chapter 2- Master the Art of Storytelling

TED talks are statistically proven most effective when delivered within 18 minutes. Within that period, you have to introduce yourself, grab your audience's attention, make them want to listen, show them how to retain your information, and persuade them to take action. TED masters have discovered that the best way to knock out most of those focal points is through telling a story. Leading to *Secret #2:* **Master the Art of Storytelling**. Say something compelling. Tell a tale that will reach your audience through their hearts and minds. A good story stimulates the brain, helping the speaker make a direct connection with the audience.

Stories break down walls of defense and establish a lasting connection. If you're able to tell a story that puts your listener in an emotionally responsive place, they'll digest your words and trust the message.

The key is a proportionate blend of ethos (credibility), logos (logic and data), and pathos (emotional appeal). Each sentence was weighed in TED's most persuasive talk, given by Bryan Stevenson. When averaged, his words weighed heavily on the pathos scale at 65% of his presentation.

Take some time to look over a recently delivered speech. Categorize each sentence according to Aristotle's three categories. If you aren't focusing the majority of your words on appealing to pathos, you need to revise your content to grasp your audience's emotions.

Stories are inspirations, referred to in "Talk Like TED" as "data with a soul". There are three types of stories used in effective presentations: personal stories, stories about other people who have learned a lesson, and stories of failure or success.

*A personal story* is a simple way to expose your vulnerabilities to the audience. Relaying a personal secret, fear, or childhood experience allows people to view you in a more relatable light. The intimidation of being a powerful CEO, executive, or other person of status is replaced by a human being having a conversation with another human.

*Stories about other people* still establish a strong sense of pathos. Speaking of how they've gone through some relatable trouble and overcome to unseen victories gives your listener hope that the same could happen for them. These can be as personal as a story about yourself, the object is to get the audience to relate to the message. Use the pathos gained from this story to lead into logos, your supporting information.

Telling behind the scenes stories *about large brands and corporations* shows how humble beginnings can one day transpire to greatness. This in itself inspires the audience to learn more. Tales of how large names like Prego were once unsuccessful and almost abandoned before taking the steps to change the way consumer interests are measured, keeps the audience hanging on to your every word. It sparks a passion within them, one that encourages them to continue listening.

If applicable, you can make your story more interesting by introducing heroes and villains. Reveal the challenge (your villain), the protagonist (brand hero), and how the townspeople will benefit from the villain's defeat. As a phenomenal speaker, you'll take your audience on an adventure, bending the rules, and taking risks. Your story will be a clear expression of your passion for the subject and will create a lasting impression between you and your audience.

# Chapter 3: Have A Conversation

When in front of a crowd, whether it's 10 or 100,000 in attendance, you need to come across as if you're having a conversation with friends. This requires hours of relentless practice, 10,000 to be exact (scientific fact).

First you'll need to enlist help with planning your words. Referring back to those passionate people you keep around you, get suggestions from your family, friends, colleagues, and even your following. Often times, you're too close to your content to attack it objectively.

Once your presentation is completed, seek as much feedback as possible. Go through live rehearsals with small audiences and ask for their opinions. In addition, record yourself and be honest about what you think. You can use your smart phone or a camera on a tripod. It doesn't have to be perfect, but you need to honestly review your mannerisms, tone, speed, and overall delivery.

Presentations need to be given at an optimum rate, volume, and pitch with the perfect amount of pauses to keep your audience tuned in. Raising and dropping your voice is the equivalent of highlighting key facts on a piece of paper. Go over your content and see how to best use these four points.

Ideally, audio books are recited between 150-160 words per minute, slightly slower than the normal rate of speech. You have to give your audience the opportunity to absorb the information. While a good presentation resembles a normal conversation, TED methods prove it has slight, but crucial differences.

Body language is one of the underlying factors between an effective TED talk and normal exchange between friends. Every movement or lack thereof, gives your audience a message. Nonverbal communication matters as much as choosing the correct tone and speed to speak. Only 7% of your message is relayed verbally, the other 93% is all nonverbal communication.

The way you move determines whether you are believable to your listeners. It differentiates between deceit and a truthful delivery. Firstly, you need to believe in what you're saying, if you don't, it'll be immediately apparent. Confidence and truthfulness are commanding qualities. Posture, eye contact, attire, and language selection shows how your point will be absorbed by your target.

Great leaders take pride in every detail of their presentation. They are dressed a little better than everyone else, they address you firmly, and make eye contact. They're calm yet precise, projecting their message through the diaphragm, leaders don't whisper or cower during presentations. Their walk, speech, and appearance all scream 'leader'.

Utilizing proper hand gestures will make your argument even stronger. They emphasize your passion and work in conjunction with the pitch of your voice. Gestures are absolutely necessary for delivering an effective TED talk. The types you use (and how frequently) are determined by what type of thinker you are.

Complex thinkers use complex gestures, which give the audience more confidence in the speaker. There are a few things to remember when incorporating gestures into your presentation.

1. **Don't be afraid to use them** - This is the easiest fix for a stiff presentation, keep your hands out of your pockets.

2. **Use gestures sparingly** - Don't go overboard with the movements. Let your gestures flow naturally and avoid choreographed motions. .

3. **Use gestures at key** moments - Save your grand gestures for the feature parts of your presentation, keeping your authentic personality and style in mind when using them.

4. **Keep your gestures within the power sphere** - Beginning at the top of your eyes, your power sphere runs to the tips of your outstretched hands, to your belly button, and ending back at your eyes. Keep your gestures and gaze within this range.

Studies show that sales strategies delivered in a more attractive, active method are much more successful, by 71%, than stale monotone deliveries. These active methods all encompassed three elements: extreme animation, broad open movements, and openly projected hand motions (open palms rather than closed fists).

You can combat *fidgeting, tapping, and jingling* by recording the first five minutes of your presentation and reviewing it for unnecessary movements. Fidgeting makes you look unsure to the audience, be sure that every gesture has a purpose.

Avoid *standing rigidly* in place by making a conscious effort to walk, move, and work the room. Movement is more than acceptable, it's welcome and expected. Practice recording your presentation and be sure to walk out of the frame every so often.

Another negative gesture is *keeping your hands in your pockets*. This fix is simple, take them out and don't put them back in. One may be acceptable as long as you're moving the other hand freely.

Perfecting your natural, conversation-style presentation takes practice. The only way to achieve this is by "faking it until you make it". Continue to practice and dig within until you've discovered your presentation comfort-zone.

# Chapter 4: Teach Me Something New

**Teach Me Something New** is *Secret #4*. Your audience is looking for something fresh and new, something they've never heard before. The human brain is naturally fond of novelty. An unfamiliar solution to an old problem is bound to grab their attention.

Learning is an addictive part of life. Each new bit of information taps into millions of years of evolution and adaptation. According to a study complete by John Medina, a developmental molecular biologist at the University of Washington School of Medicine, 99.99% of all species that have ever lived are now extinct. That means the human brain was able to adapt to its environment and survive.

Dopamine is the powerful chemical that allows the brain to save information. It's responsible for developing ways to rejuvenate struggling relationships, it's your spark of excitement and creativity. A false trigger of the neurological chemical is the cause behind drug and gambling addictions.

Making your information new and exciting will increase the dopamine levels secreted by your audience. Dopamine is highly addictive, which explains why new information gives people an intense natural high.

Step out of your shell and force the audience to alter the way they look at the world. Steve Case changed the way people used the internet with the introduction of AOL. His innovation lead him to rank number 258 on Forbes list of the richest people in America.

Even if your information is familiar, you can still present it from your own perspective, adding a unique take. All you need to do is teach at least one thing that they didn't know.

It doesn't matter if you're speaking in front of the wealthiest, most successful, most intelligent audience ever, this only increases the chances they'll be persuaded with new information.

One way to accomplish this is by exploring areas that aren't directly related to your field. Carmine Gallo speaks about the exchange between Apple and the Ritz-Carlton that taught Apple the fundamentals of customer service. As a result, Apple has set new customer service standards which are observed by a wide range of industries.

Incorporating new ideas and concepts into your presentation takes a creative mind and forward thinking. Bombard your brain with new experiences, embracing each one and forcing yourself to look at the world differently. Step outside the office and take part in new events, engage new people, and visit new places. Be sure to take those experiences and fuse them with your presentation.

You'll have to learn how to reveal ideas that have never been considered in a remarkable way. Avoid cliché phrases like "There's no I in team", don't suggest solutions that have been beaten into the dirt, they work against your ability to inspire your audience and you'll begin to lose their attention.

Instead, do something different. Gregory Berns, a neuroscientist, calls the brain "a lazy piece of meat". If you want it to view something differently, it has to be presented in a fresh and unique way. Let the natural thirst for knowledge inspire you to create that story that's never been told. Don't succumb to a defeatist mentality. There is always a new story. There will always be a new approach; you just have to come up with one.

TED keeps the brain active, giving it a constant workout. Known as the "Flynn Effect", a University of Otago political-studies professor, Dr. James Flynn has discovered that the human brain is much smarter than 50, 30, even 20 years ago. With each generation comes a rise in IQ due to greater access to education. The use of various mediums including traditional schooling and time spent online appeases people's natural thirst for knowledge. Your presentation has to appeal to these same desires.

Allow your presentation to evolve according to society's interests. "Talk Like Ted" suggests creating a Twitter friendly headline for your next speech. Identify the main thing you want your audience to understand about your topic of discussion and make your headline as specific as possible. Clearly explain your ideas in a concise way that lets your audience know exactly what they're going to get. A headline shouldn't be confused for a tagline. Taglines are too vague and don't inform the audience what they need to know or how you're going to teach it to them. Don't follow someone else's outline; create a new and refreshing masterpiece.

# Chapter 5: Deliver Jay-Dropping Moments

*Secret #5* let's you know about the importance of shocking your audience. Bring them the unexpected in an impressive and surprising moment creates an emotionally charged event and heightens the senses.

Bill Gates is famously known for a 2009 presentation when he spoke about the advances of medicines and vaccines saving the lives of children everywhere. Then, he released mosquitoes out into the crowd. Before delivering his shocking moment, he appealed to the audience's emotions using a heartfelt story of how millions of people die from malaria each year.

Headlines went crazy over his act, inflating it even larger than it was, and resulting in an increased shock factor. Out of the 18-minute TED talk, the jaw dropping moment took less than 5% of the total presentation; however it was the most memorable component of all.

Your presentation should be an emotionally charged event. Reiterating on previous facts, if you can stir your audience's emotions, you'll increase the amount of dopamine secreted in their brain and sparking their memory and ability to process your information.

Occasions that fuel emotional surges (shock, surprise, joy, sadness, wonder, fear) are significantly more memorable. Hence, the reason you can remember September 11, 2011 as if it happened yesterday and somehow manage to lose the keys that were just in your hand a few moments ago. Psychology professor, Rebecca Todd, of the University of Toronto discovered that the ease of remembering an event directly correlates to how vividly and emotionally it was experienced.

The amygdala is the region of the brain that's responsible for tagging memories. It's most active during "vivid" events. In her studies, subjects were shown negative and positive emotionally arousing photographs. A third group was given neutral pictures to look at. Two separate studies were performed. The first was 45 minutes after each group viewed their images and the second came one week later. Each resulted in the two groups who were given emotionally charged images displaying much more vivid and active memories.

Dr. Jill is a TED presenter with over 10 million views, arguably due to the "ickiness" of her message. If you watch her TED talk, you'll be treated to see a real human brain attached to a spinal cord. Within two minutes, she vaguely introduced and immediately presented her audience with the brain. Both shocking and jaw dropping, the disgust of the audience pulled at their emotions.

Steve Jobs was lovingly known as the "undisputed King of Wow". Famous for his 1997 "We See Genius" presentation after returning to Apple from a 12-year absence, he took the last two minutes of his presentation to drastically slow his speech and speak from the heart. This was a simple and effective way to charge emotions.

After introducing the iPod in 2001, Jobs gave a presentation focusing on the size of the MP3, he explained to the audience the benefits of the compact device before delivering the jaw dropping "this amazing little device holds 1,000 songs and goes right in my pocket" before removing the first ever model from his pants. In this instance, his statistic and supporting evidence was the showstopper.

Bringing the same energy, Jobs dropped jaws in his 2007 presentation introducing the iPhone as three products in one. This appealed to the element of surprise. He informed his audience that Apple would be introducing three new products. Explaining one was a wide-screen iPod, the other a revolutionary mobile phone, and finally a breakthrough in internet communications. After repeating his claims a few more times to let the anticipation build, he revealed that these were not separate devices, Apple was giving them to the world in the iPhone. The audience laughed, cheered, and applauded with eager excitement.

Your presentation should also involve a "holy smokes moment". This is the emotionally charged, "wow factor" that drives your point home. It doesn't need to be fancy, "Talk Like Ted" covers five simple methods.

1. **Props and Demos** - Nothing is more emotionally charging than a first-hand experience. Mark Shaw used props in his 2013 TED presentation on neuroscience. If he could compel the audience on a topic as complex as this,

there's nothing out there that's too difficult to incorporate props or demonstrations. A lot of presenters don't even consider using props to enhance their message. Ask yourself if your presentation can benefit from a prop? You may consider asking an outsider for their opinion as well.

2. **Unexpected and Shocking Statistics** - Virtually all of the most popular TED presentations contain data, statistics, or some form of numerical information. Concrete and factual results reinforce your message. The more shocking and unexpected, the more you'll grab your audience's attention. Using these, you'll reach the person's head and heart at the same time. When presenting data, never leave it dangling. Your context is just as important as the facts being presented. Package your shocking statistic in a way that gives the greatest impact and value to the reader.

3. **Pictures, Images, and Videos** – Raghava KK delivered a talk to a TED audience in which he used brainwaves to manipulate art in real time. While speaking, he wore a biofeedback headset that recorded his brain's activity. Connected to a computer that would display the images, he presented an image he named "Mona Lisa 2.0" with his actual brain activity creating the border around the photo. He shocked the audience even more by explaining how his different state of mind (attentive, meditative, focused) altered the woman's expression. When he was angry, her frown intensified. Visuals can thrill your audience and captivate their attention.

4. **Memorable Headlines**- Stewart Brand presented a brazen prediction in a 2013 TED talk which he proposed the possibility of reviving animals that are now extinct. *"We will get wooly mammoths back."* This statement is better known as a sound bite or a short, provocative phrase

that can be repeated and is likely to be retweeted and posted on social media. It's critical to getting newspapers and television to accept and share your story. The sound bite has such a great impact that TED has devoted a complete Twitter handle (@TEDQuote) and website to the most popular quotes from TED speakers.

5. **Personal Stories** – Stories are so important, an entire chapter was dedicated to them and they still need to be mentioned again. To be a great communicator, you must know the art of storytelling. This is the most profound way to create an impact and capture your audience's attention. Even as an executive, it's important to let down your guard and expose something that will assist your audience in seeing you differently. Present "new" information that will make the audience connect to you emotionally, outside of the intimidating persona of expert, professional, or CEO.

Finally, you should end your presentation on a high-note. Some "mind-blowing" moment for the audience to take home with them. This can be as exaggerate as a stunt or as simple as an emotional story. To make the most of your presentation, you need at least one jaw-dropping moment.

# Chapter 6: Lighten Up

The most popular presentation in TED history isn't a likely selection. Sir Ken Robinson spoke on the effects of schooling, how it kills creativity. In 18 minutes, he delivered a presentation that drew in over 15 million views. His words on education reform outshine people who are more famous and have a greater following, yet none of these presentations even come close to the response Robinson received. The main reason is that his TED talk was funny. This "Talk Like TED" *Secret #6:* **Lighten Up** – don't take yourself too seriously.

Robinson strategically created a presentation that made his audience think and laugh at the same time – he mainly used stories. He told stories about a little girl who was drawing in class and silenced her teacher's opinions. When asked, "What are you drawing?" the little girl replied, "I'm drawing a picture of God." The teacher came back and said, "But nobody knows what God looks like." The 6-year-old answered, "They will in a minute."

Throughout the duration of his speech, he delivered thought provoking words that pulled at your emotions. All of which treated him to a prolonged standing ovation. Humor is a key tool for the most successful speakers in the world, however it must be used appropriately. Overused, rude, or dirty jokes aren't going to benefit your message. In contrast, a relevant, humorous observation is perfect.

A Berkeley-based research company studied the effects humor has on the brain. Through neurological research, they discovered that people watch and buy what they like based on humor.

At the first meeting, the brain naturally starts to form impressions and judge the other person. You'll determine characteristics of their personality including whether you perceive them to be friendly and trustworthy. Humor is the best form of interpersonal communication, it's a social skill that is sought after and admired by others.

Humor is vital in more than just the TED stage. It is an asset in your personal relationships and business settings as well. If used skillfully, it'll disarm the defensive and deflect criticism. The ability to make someone laugh relieves tension and immediately improves morale, allowing you to communicate difficult messages.

The best way to be humorous is not to try at all. It sounds counterproductive at first but unauthentic humor is easily detected. Avoid jokes, no matter how funny you think they are, unless you're a professional comedian in your prime.

1. *Anecdotes, stories, and observations* are the most fluid method of incorporating humor into your presentation. Think objectively about things and events that have made you and your colleagues laugh. If they're appropriate and have a proven rate of success, it's probably safe to use them with your audience.

2. *Analogies and metaphors* are another thought provoking way to make your audience laugh. Comparing similarities between two different things is a rhetorical technique used to explain complex topics. For example, Intel compared data with sand to show how much data the world will have by the year 2020 (57 times more than every grain in the world). "Where in the heck are we going to store all of that information?" He created a shock factor, excitement, and made his audience laugh at the same time.

3. *A quote* is an easy way to get your audience to laugh, especially if you're having difficulty coming up with humorous situations of your own. They can come from someone famous, a person in your family, or even an anonymous person. Quotes also break up presentations in your slides, giving your audience a creative mental break.

Do some extra work when researching your quotes. Don't rely only on famous people or well-known, over used quotes. Find ones that will lighten the mood and alleviate the complexity of your topic. Often, you can use quotes from people you know that made you laugh or grabbed your attention.

4. *Video* is seldom used in presentations, even TED talks, but it is an effective way to use humor to your advantage. It also takes some of the pressure off you since you won't need to be funny on the spot. In a presentation on Apple Stores and customer service, Carmine Gallo plays a video of a comedian who's out to see how much he can get away with in some of Apple's chains. Once he brings in a goat, in another he orders a pizza to be delivered to the store,

and he even hired a small band to play a personal song for an intimate dance with he and his wife. This enhanced the message that Apple's employees are trained not to sell "stuff", instead their mission is to enhance people's lives.

5. Comedians test jokes on different audiences to gauge their response, the same goes for *photos and stories*. Alone, the text of a story can be appreciated but when accompanied by supporting visuals, you'll be able to include additional senses and appeal to the audience's emotions. A funny story plus a humorous photo creates a more vividly memorable moment in your presentation. Photos are perfect for lightening up the sterile appearance of PowerPoint presentations. You'll incorporate an emotional impact for your audience.

These five techniques can all be used congruently in a presentation. If you're not the naturally humorous one, or if you're aiming for a good smile not a hearty laugh, there's a way to do that with each one of them.

Humor allows you to introduce complex topics to those who are not familiar with the subject. It also deflects controversial topics and allows relief from traumatic events. It involves a bit of risk, but it's worth the effort. The businesses that ignore the impact of a humorous presentation usually produce a boring final product that yields minimal results.

# Chapter 7: Stick to the 18-Minute Rule

Professor Larry Smith usually gives his students three-hour lectures. His November 2011 TED talk lasted only 15-minutes, but it was viewed over 1.5 million times. Condensing his thoughts into such a short segment was a challenge but, for some reason, it was amazingly successful.

TED presentations have been analyzed and 18-minutes is a solid rule to follow. *Secret #7:* **Stick to the 18-Minute Rule** because researchers have identified that an information overload or "cognitive backlog" prohibits the transfer and comprehension of ideas. If you must exceed 18 minutes, be sure to incorporate soft breaks with stories, videos, and demonstrations every 10 minutes.

It works similarly to Twitter's character limits. It forces speakers to analyze their message and condense it to the core, most impacting information. Listening, although it requires little to no physical involvement, is a draining activity. All forms of cognitive processing, including thinking, speaking, and listening, are silently demanding on the physical. To listen requires the audience to constantly absorb information and retain it to memory.

Overloading their "cognitive backlog" risks upsetting your audience. The longer you speak, the more you force them to organize, comprehend, and memorize your information. They'll get frustrated or, even worse, they can grow angry.

The brain is easily tired and it takes an excessive amount of energy to listen and learn. Similar to the exhaustion after the first day of a new job or once you've completed hours of studying, a long lecture will eventually cause your audience to drift away, unless you incorporate those soft breaks every 10 minutes.

The 18-20 minute golden threshold is a constraint that works in partnership with the creative parts of the mind. It's not too short and not too long, the perfect length of time to effectively persuade your audience. Using former President Kennedy's 15-minute inaugural speech as an example, it's possible to briefly deliver powerful information.

Even if you feel there's no way to condense your speech into such a short time frame, it's best to try it anyway. "The Laws of Subtraction" by Matthew May speak on the benefits of being creatively pushed to your limits. Establishing boundaries for your presentation provides a targeted focus and forces your creativity to thrive under the pressure. Selecting which information to subtract is often more important than the information that is left.

According to Albert Einstein, "If you can't explain it simply, you don't understand it well enough." David Christian chose to tackle a topic as broad as "the history of the world" and delivered his entire narrative in 17 minutes and 40 seconds. As the teacher of a world history course that covers the complete history of the universe, he knew the subject inside and out. Present your information in a sophisticated, short, and simple manner.

Understanding the "rule of three" will help you organize and condense your information. Neil Pasricha shares the "The Three A's of Awesome": attitude, awareness, and authenticity. How you deal with life's challenges, being aware that there was once a time when everything around you was new to you, and being accepting of who you are and what you offer are three qualities that will take you very far.

This leads to Pasricha's understanding of the rule of three, a theory stating that the human brain can only digest three bits of information in the short-term memory. The more items that are added, the less likely the information will be retained. It's like remembering a phone number, most likely, you'll commit it to memory through chunks, the three digit number and the last four digits.

When writing and speaking, three is the most satisfying number to use. It got President Barack Obama elected with his phrase, "Yes we can,". The world's most famous brands utilize the number. Names like ING, UPS, IBM, CNN, and BBC.

TED talks also happen in threes. Kevin Allocca is a YouTube trends manager who's popular presentation showcased three main points in a 10-minute presentation. Many other TED presenters use three stories throughout their message.

You can build your own message map in three simple steps:
1. Create a Twitter-Friendly Headline
2. Support Your Headline with Three Messages
3. Reinforce Each Message with Stories, Statistics, and Examples.

"Talk Like TED" gives you a blank template to use when creating your message map, but be sure to stick to the 18-minute rule.

# Chapter 8: Paint a Mental Picture with Multisensory Experiences

*Secret #8* informs you on the importance of delivering presentations with components that touch more than one of the senses. Appealing to at least two creates an exciting environment more conducive to learning. It enhances points made earlier regarding the brains tendency to ignore common experiences in favor of vividly stimulating ones. The brain craves new information and multisensory experiences.

You can accomplish this with multimedia. A combination of text, animation, photographs, and video always yields a more intense recollection of information. The blend of audio and visual presentations is even effective with those who are unfamiliar with the information.

When creating presentations, it's better to use images in place of text whenever possible. The combination of pictures and written text is easier to recall than text solely. Of all the senses, vision is the most profound, which is why many presenters devote a large portion of their presentation to visual appeal. This method has captivated TED audiences worldwide for 30 years.

Al Gore is well-known for delivering multimedia presentations in his effort to raise awareness surrounding climate changes. His passion and delivery have received raving reviews from some of the country's most successful entrepreneurs and executives.

Producer Laurie David explained his message as the most clear and powerful explanation she's ever seen. She was inspired because she felt his delivery was more like a movie than a presentation. If he'd only read his text, void of any visuals, Gore would not have made the same impact.

Al Gore's professionally designed images among other popular TED speakers are ending the way PowerPoint is known forever. The traditional slide has 40 words, the occasional bullet points, and a stock image. This is too much and too cluttered. Replacing words with powerful pictures and using text as a minimal enhancement makes a stronger impact.

The ability to multitask and pay sound attention while retaining information is non-existent. To ask your audience to listen to what you're saying while reading a slide full of information is dangerous. You risk overwhelming them, losing their attention, or worse, devaluing your message because of missed information.

"The History of Our World in 18 Minutes" is a visual experience that plays on the senses. As soon as David Christian walked on stage, he introduced a video. The first two and a half minutes of the presentation contained no text on any of his slides. The remainder of his speech was creatively comprised of supporting context. Reviewers appreciated the multisensory experience, calling it "engaging", "amazing", and "stunning".

You can take notes from Photographer Chris Jordan who used photos of Barbie dolls to convey his message. Beginning with an image of 50 Barbies placed in circular patterns, he advanced to a larger version of thousands of dolls. If you hadn't seen the first, you would've thought it was a floral painting. Lastly, utilizing the power of three, Jordan switched to an image of 32,000 Barbie dolls stating this was the number of women who undergo breast augmentation surgery each month, most of whom are under 21. Rather than simply presenting a chart of the statistic, Jordan created an emotional visual image for his audience.

If presenting pie charts and other tables or graphs, you can still stimulate the senses by adding background images. When using PowerPoint, you should not exceed 40 words in the first 10 slides. Instead, tell a story that engages your audience with each word. TED's greatest presenters avoid the use of bullet points at all. They're the least memorable way of presenting information. Get creative, your audience will love it.

Visuals are important but it's also wise to appeal to an additional sense. Hearing is usually the most complimentary due to the impact of the pitch, rate, volume, intensity, and articulation of your words.

Lisa Kristine developed a powerful TED presentation that used only photographs and profound narration for the first two minutes. She was able to create a "visual imprint on a person's mind." The brain's visual cortex can't tell the difference between real and imaginary. If you can vividly think of something, the areas of the brain associated with it are activated as if you're really seeing it.

Janine Shepherd created a mental picture without using pictures at all. Playing on the brain's inability to decipher the difference between reality and the imagination, she told the story of the bike ride that changed her life. Her evocative and visually descriptive choice of words brought the audience into the moment with her.

Musicians are also skilled in taking you on a journey through their words. Lyrics invoke emotions, which is the key aspect of gaining your audience's attention. The focus of your presentation should be around taking your audience to another place. Create a fascinating story, intriguing characters, and relevant props.

Advance from the reliance on slides to deliver your message. You can introduce a product, perform a demonstration, or ask for audience participation.

# Chapter 9: Stay In Your Lane

Be authentic, open, and transparent in your interactions. Most people can spot when someone isn't genuine. Attempting to portray the image of someone or something you're not is going to discredit your entire message.

Throughout "Talk Like TED", you're instructed on all the technical sequences and science behind developing an effective TED presentation, however public speaking is an art form. You have to speak from the heart, it'll be appreciated by your audience.

Take notes from the famous TED speakers and other professionals you admire. To make a lasting impression, you must create a lane for yourself and leave your unique stamp on the world.

Tell those stories that expose a few vulnerabilities, allow people to see that you're human and experience the same doubts, troubles, and challenges as they have. Take your content and test it with friends or family members before expressing it to your audience. This will enable you to speak from a more genuine approach. Surrounding by the ones you love and trust, you'll gain confidence and lose your nervousness.

Insecurities around public speaking are shared with some of the world's greatest communicators. Joel Osteen is an internationally famous pastor who admitted his first sermon in October 1999 scared him to death. Just ten years later, he found himself preaching to a sold out Yankee Stadium.

Perfecting the craft takes years of experience and hours of practice. You have to be willing to invest the necessary time. The things you do on a daily basis soon come as a force of habit because you do them so often. When you get out of your car, you lock the door. Even if you don't remember the action, it's done because you've committed days, months, and years to practicing it. Repetition allows the mind to roam freely so you'll present your story openly and genuinely.

Corporate leaders worth billions of dollars experience the same apprehension as those developing startup businesses. It's a natural reaction; however with passion, knowledge, and practice you'll be able to master the art.

From now on, your presentations will be compared to the best of TED speakers. Utilizing these nine secrets, your audience will immediately notice a refreshing change in your delivery. Your revised style will now inspire them and lift their spirits. They'll leave your presentation thinking and feeling differently.

TED presentations have acquired over one billion global views via the TED website, YouTube, and they're embedded in endless blogs. TED presenters are even improving on their delivery and performance. This innovative style is renaming the way an audience expects a presenter to deliver their message. It's becoming a culture shared with each of TED's masterful presenters. Find your passion and develop an authentic creation with your message and your audience. As long as you stay in your lane and be true to yourself, the world will welcome you with open arms.

# Thanks for Reading

Hello, this message is from the readers and writers at Summary Station. We hope that you enjoyed this summary/analysis and that it has helped your life in some way. It is our intention to create information that our readers will find useful and valuable.

We fell grateful for the opportunity to have people read our books and we are even more grateful when our customers leave a review. Please leave a review that lets us know what you liked about this book so that we can work on improving future books. Thanks again for your time.

# About Summary Station

Many great books are released every year and most avid readers know that they never have time to read all of the books on their list. In today's world many people do not get as much time to read as they would like, so it is important to use any reading time wisely. The problem with this is that it can be very difficult to know if a book is worth reading until you have already invested some time into reading it.

This is one of the many reasons that Summary Station was created. The staff at Summary Station wants to provide readers with a way to get a good idea of a book before they invest their time and money into reading it. We make sure to provide you with as much information about a book as we possibly can, without giving away the ending or any other crucial spoilers.

With Summary Station you can be assured that you will not only get a quality summary of a featured book, but you will also receive valuable information and analysis. The themes and characters are discussed in each summary as well as a brief review of the featured book. Even if you know you are going to definitely read a book, it will give you a big advantage in understanding the book if you explore one of our excellent summaries first.

# Preview of "Summary and Analysis of "The Slight Edge" by Jeff Olson""

In the first chapter, Jeff Olson introduces his readers to the idea that every single person on this planet has the potential to either turn into a poor, unsuccessful beach bum, or into a successful entrepreneur with a huge balance on his bank account. He tells his own story – about how he went from failure to success to another failure, and how he slowly learned that failure and success both happen for the same reason, and that this one single reason can either work for or against you, depending on how you use it. The reader is motivated by reading on because they would like to know more about the idea that people have complete control about the direction their life is taking.

Many readers of "The Slight Edge" will have read other self help and personal development books. Many of those books promise to hold the secret to success and to a happy life. Mr. Olson describes how most people who buy such books find the ideas intriguing and apply them for a while. But then they stop and complain about all the techniques not working. He explains that all the wanting, wishing, and positive thinking in the world does not help people with achieving their goals unless they have "the first ingredient" to success.

Jeff Olson takes away the belief that failure is not an option, and that positive thinking and wishing is all you need. He mentions a variety of examples of famous people who only came to their success after many failures (e.g. Edison and his light bulb). He explains that the missing ingredient to success is a person's own philosophy, i.e. the attitude behind their actions.

The right philosophy leads a person to the right attitude, the right actions, and the right results. This results in a good, successful life. While the wrong philosophy leads to the opposite.

The lesson from chapter 2 is nicely summarized in a quote within the chapter:

"Success is the progressive realization of a worthy ideal. Successful people do what unsuccessful people are not willing to do."

## [Click Here To Check Out The Rest Of The Book](#)

# Check Out More Books By Summary Station

**"A Fine and Dangerous Season" by Keith Raffel – Summary**

**"The Slight Edge" by Jeff Olson - Summary**

**"America: Imagine A World Without Her" by Dinesh D'Souza - Summary**

**"Long Knives" by Charles Rosenberg – Summary**

"The Bird Eater" by Ania Ahlborn – Summary

"Flash Boys: A Wall Street Revolt" by Michael Lewis - Summary

"The Doctors Diet" by Travis Storks – Summary

"I Can See Clearly Now" by Dr. Wayne Dyer - Summary

"Think Like A Freak: The Authors of Freakonomics Offer to Retrain Your Brain" by Steven D. Levitt and Stephen J. Dubner - Summary

**"Wheat Belly: Lose the Wheat, Lose the Weight, and Find your Path Back to Health" by William Davis M.D. - Summary**

**"The Confidence Code: The Science and Art of Self-Assurance – What Women Should Know" by Katty Kay and Claire Shipman - Summary**

**"Everything is Bullshit: The Greatest Scams on Earth Revealed" by Priceonomics - Summary**

Wake Tech. Libraries
9101 Fayetteville Road
Raleigh, North Carolina 27603-5696

**DATE DUE**

GAYLORD     PRINTED IN U.S.A.

WITHDRAWN